"Happy Fifty(ieth)"

Joyce

Colin

Gwen

Marion

Ken

Ira

Anne

Doug

Bill

Terry

Pat

May 21st. 1992.

Two Spirits Soar

BOY PLAYING WITH DOG   *1982*   *Acrylic on canvas*   *60.96 cm x 91.44 cm (24" x 36")*   *Allen Sapp Paintings Inc.*

The little boy is enjoying playing with his dog. Soon it will be time to go into the house and the horse taken to shelter.

Two Spirits Soar

THE ART OF ALLEN SAPP

The Inspiration of Allan Gonor

W. P. KINSELLA

First published in 1990 by
Stoddart Publishing Co. Limited
34 Lesmill Road
Toronto, Canada
M3B 2T6

CANADIAN CATALOGUING IN PUBLICATION DATA

Kinsella, W. P.
Two spirits soar: the art of Allen Sapp, the inspiration of Allan Gonor

ISBN 0-7737-2427-3

1. Sapp, Allen, 1929-   – Criticism and interpretation.   2. Cree Indians in art.
3. Indians of North America – Canada – Pictorial works.   4. Gonor, Allan – Influence.   I. Title.

ND249.S3K5 1990   759.11   C90-094000-X

DESIGN: Brant Cowie / ArtPlus Limited

COLOUR PHOTOGRAPHY: Zach Hauser

Printed and bound in Hong Kong by Book Art, Toronto.

Painting on title page:
PEOPLE PASSING BY   *1988   Acrylic on canvas   45.72 cm x 60.96 cm (18" x 24")   Allen Sapp Paintings Inc.*
(Comments on paintings throughout are by the artist.)

CONTENTS

POW-WOW DANCERS   *1987*   *Acrylic on canvas*   *101.6 cm x 152.4 cm (40" x 60")*   *Allen Sapp Paintings Inc.*

There are many dancers at this pow-wow, all dressed in fancy costumes. Many have come a long way and they meet old friends.

MAKING A CRAZY QUILT   *1974   Acrylic on canvas   60.96 cm x 91.44 cm (24" x 36")   Allen Sapp Gallery — The Gonor Collection*

Nokum is making a crazy quilt with bright colours. Her grandchild stands at the door.

THE ARTIST
AND THE WRITER

THERE ARE STORIES of viewers being moved to tears by the art of Allen Sapp. I can verify that those stories are not exaggerated. When I first saw Allen Sapp's work, not in person, but photographs of his paintings, they touched my heart as no works of art had ever done before. I have visited famous art museums, seen world-renowned masterpieces, and though I recognized and appreciated their quality, and in some cases their beauty, no works of art ever totally moved me until I saw Allen Sapp's paintings.

Many art lovers who have never experienced the world of Allen Sapp are attracted to his work and moved by the exotic locations and subject matter of his paintings, but it was the familiarity of Allen's paintings that touched me.

What immediately impressed me was that Allen had exactly reproduced prairie scenes that were also stored in my memory, scenes so real that they quickly transported me back to my childhood on a remote homestead in Northern Alberta. The landscapes of the paintings, the backgrounds of poplar and birch trees, the prairie grasses, the winter skies were so accurate, so much as I remembered them, that I developed an instant attachment to the paintings, a longing to own them.

I didn't doubt that other people could share my memories, but how could Allen Sapp reproduce those memories so perfectly? So accurately that I could smell the rich red clover hay on the hayrack, the strong scent of horses as they pulled a wagon over a snow-covered field.

THE CROP IS PRETTY GOOD   *1982*   *Acrylic on canvas*   *60.96 cm x 91.44 cm (24" x 36")*   *Allen Sapp Paintings Inc.*

The harvest is good, and there are many workers in the field. It is important to get the work done before the snow comes.

POW-WOW DRUMMERS   *1989   Acrylic on canvas   91.44 cm x 152.4 cm (36" x 60")   Allen Sapp Paintings Inc.*
The drummers are very important for a pow-wow. They sing and make the music that others will dance to.

Looking at other paintings, I could hear the sounds of the harness, and the rumbling of the wagon wheels jolting across the prairie, or the sounds of snow crushed beneath the runners of a sleigh. Just by looking at Allen's paintings I could smell the freshness of a spring thaw, hear the snow squeaking underfoot, hear the bite of the ax felling a tree, smell the bitter odor of bark and pine sap in the air, hear the horses shaking their harness, making breathy, trembly noises as they pulled a load of logs or hay.

Over the years, as I've come to think more about Allen Sapp's work, as I've been lucky enough to own a few of his paintings, I've come to realize that though he and I work in different mediums of artistic expression, we do substantially the same thing. Allen works with paint on canvas while I work with a typewriter or word processor on paper, but we both employ the senses — sight, sound, taste, touch, smell — to make our viewers or readers experience the pictures and stories we want them to enjoy.

THOUGH I HAD BEEN FAMILIAR with his paintings for a number of years, I didn't meet Allen Sapp until the fall of 1978. I had recently returned to Canada after several years of graduate study in Iowa City, Iowa, and soon after my arrival I discovered that Allen was having an exhibition at the Gainsborough Gallery in Calgary. Even though I knew it would be painful to look at a gallery full of his paintings and not be able to afford one, I wanted to see his work, and since he was going to be appearing at the gallery, I wanted to try to convey to him, in person, how much his work meant to me.

First in Victoria, British Columbia, and later in Iowa City, when I was striving to provide realistic description for the fictional stories I set on an Indian reserve near Hobbema, Alberta, I had often stared at photographs of Allen Sapp's paintings, trying to find the right words to translate the essence of his painted scenes to the pages of manuscript. I was seldom successful, at least to my satisfaction. Several months before my return to Canada and Calgary, I had published my first book, a collection of seventeen stories, *Dance Me Outside*.

I decided that to show my appreciation, I would take a copy of *Dance Me Outside*, sign it personally to Allen Sapp, and deliver it to him at the Gainsborough Gallery.

That afternoon is the first time I saw an Allen Sapp painting up close, and I was overwhelmed with the spirit his work conveyed, with how much more wonderful the paintings were in reality than in mere photographs. I was also overcome by envy of the rich Calgarians who walked about nonchalantly plucking the tags from paintings that were selling for more than my net worth as of that day.

Allen Sapp was very busy signing books and accepting good wishes, but when he was finally alone for a moment, I approached, shook his hand, and offered the signed copy of my book.

"I try to do with words on paper what you do so wonderfully on canvas," I said. "I'd like you to have a copy of my book, and I hope you enjoy it."

Allen said a simple thank-you, and I retreated.

What a shock when, less than a minute later, I overheard a nearby conversation.

"You know Allen Sapp is illiterate," the female voice said.

"Is that right?" said her companion.

"Oh, he signs his name on the paintings, and he'll sign an inscription on his book (*A Cree Life: The Art of Allen Sapp*) but only if you print out what you want said. He can copy the inscription, but he can't read or write."

I wished I could shrink and slip out under the door of the gallery, never to be seen again. For what is the stupidest gift one could give an illiterate man? A book, right?

I crept out of the gallery, looking over my shoulder, hoping no one had noticed what I had done. Hoping Allen Sapp would forgive me such a crass social blunder.

But the incident had a happy ending.

A few weeks later, I received a warm letter from Dr. Allan Gonor, of North Battleford, Saskatchewan, saying that Allen Sapp had brought the book to him, and that Dr. Gonor had read it and loved it, and had read a good part of it aloud to Allen, who also enjoyed my stories.

Dr. Gonor invited me to visit him anytime I was passing through North Battleford. He was so enthusiastic about my writing that he ordered numerous copies of *Dance Me Outside* to send to friends of his all around the world.

THE SUN DANCE   *1987   Acrylic on canvas   101.6 cm x 152.4 cm (40" x 60")   Allen Sapp Paintings Inc.*
The Sun Dance is very important to my people. It has a spiritual meaning that makes us feel good.

PEOPLE GETTING TOGETHER FOR SUN DANCE   *1987   Acrylic on canvas   60.96 cm x 91.44 cm (24" x 36")   Private collection*
Many people who used to come to the Sun Dance set up their teepees and slept and cooked in them. Now a lot of people have campers and tents instead.

Allen Sapp and Allan Gonor at the launch of A Cree Life: The Art of Allan Sapp, *1977*

I didn't realize how lucky I was, for though I knew Dr. Gonor was Allen Sapp's mentor, I didn't realize to what extent the Gonors had been responsible for launching Allen's career. Dr. Gonor began to promote my books with the same wholehearted enthusiasm he had always had for Allen's paintings. And my mail soon began to reflect that promotion, for I received letters from readers far and wide, saying they had been given a book by Dr. Gonor, or that Dr. Gonor or one of his friends had recommended my fiction with such spirit that they had gone out and bought my book.

I met Dr. Gonor the next fall, when Allen Sapp had another showing in Calgary. He was a charming, caring, hyperactive whirlwind of a man, a man genuinely interested in other people, generous with his time and resources. The next time my wife, Ann, and I were driving through North Battleford, we telephoned and were invited to the Gonors' house for the evening and shown the dozens of Allen Sapp paintings in their beautiful home, as well as their large collection of Eskimo art.

What a thrill it was for my wife and me to sleep in a bedroom with eleven Allen Sapp paintings on the walls. We counted them before we went to bed, happy as kids in a candy store.

Because the Gonors were so generous toward me with their time and in their praise of my writing, each time we visited them in North Battleford, I tried to have some new manuscript with me to read to them, and to Dr. Gonor's ever-present tape recorder. It was the least I could do for someone who was so genuinely interested in all forms of creative work, so overflowing with human kindness. Dr. Gonor made the road to success a little easier for me, and I will always be grateful.

On another memorable occasion, again when Allen Sapp had a show at Gainsborough Gallery in Calgary, Ann and I spent the afternoon at the gallery with Ruth and Allan Gonor and Sapp. By this time Allen's work was so popular that when the gallery opened to the public (there had been a long line outside), there was a positive crush of oil-rich Calgarians running about tearing the tags off the fifty or so paintings available. The rush was such that two women who wanted the same painting became engaged in a furious battle, complete with screaming and hair-pulling, a battle that eventually had to be settled in court.

Dr. Gonor loved cameras, and often carried a movie camera in addition to the one or more still cameras that hung from straps around his neck. This particular afternoon — it was just after my fourth book, *Born Indian*, had been published — Dr. Gonor took endless photographs of Allen Sapp and me and various combinations of the four of us in the gallery, in front of several of Allen's paintings, with Allen holding my new book, with me holding the book. Finally, he herded Allen and me outdoors, and repeated the round of photographs.

Neither Allen nor I have much enthusiasm for this sort of thing, but Dr. Gonor was so vital, so energetic, so thrilled to be a part of our accomplishments that there was no way we could say no.

After what must have been the hundredth photograph, while Dr. Gonor was busy changing film in one of his cameras, Allen Sapp leaned over to me and whispered, with a straight face, "I expect our souls are gone by now."

MANY CREATIVE PEOPLE seem to have had particularly lonely childhoods, to have been cast as the outsider by their peers, to have been physically disadvantaged, inept at sports, picked on by contemporaries. All of the above certainly seems to have been the case with both Allen Sapp and myself, and in this regard I want to try to explore those similarities to see if our backgrounds and life experiences had any profound effects on our choices to live by our creative wits.

I was born on an isolated homestead in Northern Alberta, an only child, over-protected by my parents who were fearful that something would happen to me because my father had experienced poor health for most of his life. He had suffered from tuberculosis, at least partially as an aftermath of being gassed in France during the First World War. The nearest neighbours were a mile away, the nearest children more than three miles away. Our only transportation was by horse-drawn wagon in the summer or sleigh in winter. Consequently, having no contact with other children, I grew up acting like and thinking of myself as a small adult.

NICE DAY TO SLIDE   *1988   Acrylic on canvas   76.2 cm x 101.6 cm (30" x 40")   Allen Sapp Paintings Inc.*
Little children didn't have any fancy toys. They liked playing outside and sliding on a home-made sleigh.

WILL BE MAKING TEA SOON   *1985   Acrylic on canvas   60.96 cm x 91.44 cm (24" x 36")   Allen Sapp Paintings Inc.*
In the summer the men sat around talking and telling stories, and the children played. Then someone would say it's time to make tea soon.

Allen Sapp being held by his mother

Maggie Soonias, Allen's grandmother, and her brother

Though tall, I was thin and sickly as a child, and when we moved to Edmonton in 1945 I found I was unable to fit in with children my own age because I lacked basic skills to socialize and to play in groups, as well as having no ability or experience in sports of any kind. I was totally inept at team sports, softball, soccer, and gymnastics, and this lack of competence brought me no end of scorn from my athletic contemporaries. I grew up not knowing how to skate or swim or ride a bicycle, abilities that are totally unimportant in adult life, but those by which pre-teen children are often rated by their peers.

Since I had been brought up in an isolated rural area, entirely around adults, skating, swimming, bike riding, and competitive sports of all kinds had no place in my life until I was thrust into school in the city at age eleven. By then I felt it was too late to even attempt to acquire those skills.

I was always the last one picked for any sports team, and because I was looked down on and wasn't expected to perform, I didn't, not even bothering to try. Even today, I still don't relate well in group situations and still feel a bit of an outsider as a result of my unorthodox upbringing.

Growing up alone, I became adept at creating games to amuse myself. Later, when I had actual playmates, I found much of their play boring, and I particularly disliked that they had no tolerance or respect for silence, always having to be doing something, saying something. I was often much happier playing alone, accompanied by the fictitious friends I had invented as playmates.

I told my imaginary friends stories, and I created stories for them to tell me.

I was considered odd by my contemporaries, while really all I wanted was to be left alone, which I never was, for children can be very cruel to anyone who doesn't conform to what they consider normal behaviour. They seem to seek out anyone whom they regard as different, in order to torment that person.

Allen Sapp, in spite of maturing into a large, well-built adult, was small and sickly as a child. In early photographs he is smaller than his younger brothers. In fact he was so sickly that after his mother died of tuberculosis, he was sent to live with his beloved grandmother, Maggie Soonias, or Nokum, who tried to improve his health by treating him with Indian herbs and medicines.

Allen Sapp (second from left) with his father, Alex, and brother John (upper left), brothers Henry and Simon (front row left to right), and sister, Stella

His grandmother was about the only one who didn't consider him odd for spending his time drawing. Many of Allen's early works of art, the interior scenes in her cabin at Red Pheasant Reserve, are painted from the point of view of someone lying in a bed, since Allen, during his pre-teen years, was confined to bed for great lengths of time, suffering from meningitis.

Even after my family moved to Edmonton, I was seriously ill on a number of occasions, near death once with strep throat, just as Allen nearly died of meningitis. During my long convalescences I spent my time creating stories, much more comfortable alone than in school or playing with contemporaries who tended to ridicule everything I did.

My life in general has, of course, been much easier than Allen Sapp's. I endured the indifference and sometime hostility of peers, and a high school counsellor who gave me bad advice, stating that I should not pursue a career as a writer (even though I had scored ninety-eight percent in the writing section of an aptitude test and zero percent in the mechanical section). He advised me to go to university to obtain a degree in engineering or accounting (two subjects I possessed no aptitude for or interest in) and then write as a hobby. But Allen, during his stay at Onion Lake School in Saskatchewan, besides not being accepted by his peers, was subjected to the white man's religion and discipline and was forbidden to speak in Cree, his native tongue. Allen was also ridiculed for his single-minded interest in drawing, and for ignoring all other aspects of school in favour of his art.

I wasn't as single-minded as Allen, and I regret that I wasn't. Seventeen-year-olds are impressionable, and I half-believed my guidance counsellor — I didn't go to university then, but I held a series of evil jobs, ranging from civil servant to taxi driver, to pizza maker, to repo man, for about fifteen years. These jobs took too much out of me to leave any time for serious writing, though if anyone had asked, which they didn't, I always considered myself a writer.

Allen recalls, "One thing that really hurt me. If I talk in Cree there at Onion Lake School, I'm in trouble. I can't go to the picture show. It's a good show. *Rodeo*, a good one. Because I talk Cree now I'm in trouble. They put me away to that bedroom; I can't go to the show.

TAKING HORSES INTO THE BARN   *1982   Acrylic on canvas   60.96 cm x 91.44 cm (24" x 36")   Allen Sapp Paintings Inc.*
The day's work is over. It is getting dark and the horses are taken into the barn for shelter and to be fed and watered.

ASKING THE MAN WHAT HE WANTS TO DO   *1982   Acrylic on canvas   60.96 cm x 91.44 cm (24" x 36")   Allen Sapp Paintings Inc.*

It is a nice summer day and a neighbour drops over to see his friend. He wonders what to do today.

"And you know what happened to me in the bedroom? I was in pain, hurt. I want to see that stampede."

More important, the artist might say to his detractors, the things that you're good at — sports, contests of strength — will soon be completely irrelevant to your lives, while what I'm doing will carry me for a lifetime. I just have to wait it out.

But that waiting it out was a trying experience for Allen Sapp and for me. We faced and overcame the impossibility of doing something different in a society where anything different is ridiculed.

ALLEN AND I BOTH had strong family ties. His grandmother gave Allen rules to live by, and her influence on him was strong enough that he followed those rules: no cards, no alcohol, respect for the rights and property of others. To Allen, cards mean gambling, and he avoided playing card games of any kind. He is also a life-long non-drinker, and managed, even when very poor, to avoid trouble with the law. I've followed much the same path, though cards are not anathema to me — they are a pastime, and I have no time to pass; if I'm not travelling or working I have reading to catch up on. There are not enough hours in the day as it is.

Alcohol has never been a problem for me. Even before I became diabetic in 1982 and a total abstainer, I would have a beer about twice a year. I have never liked the taste of alcohol, and have never understood how anyone could have a craving for it. Though Allen and I smoked when we were younger, both of us gave up the habit many years ago.

Allen always considered himself a painter and I always considered my self a writer, but success came late for us — we were each in our mid-thirties before we achieved any financial rewards for our work, and in each case it was contact with a mentor that precipitated our eventual success.

In my case the mentor was fiction writer W. D. Valgardson. At age thirty-five, I decided to attend the University of Victoria full-time and work toward a degree in Creative Writing. My writing skills improved. I graduated in 1973 with a B.A. in Creative Writing, still publishing infrequently, and though I knew I was writing stories that were ninety percent publishable, I couldn't get that final ten percent that was the difference between occasional publication and outright success.

In the fall of 1974, Valgardson, a young Manitoba writer, came to teach fiction writing at the University of Victoria. I admired his first book, *Bloodflowers*, very much and decided to go back to take a course with him, even though I had already graduated.

That writing course changed my life.

Bill Valgardson took the first stories I submitted to him and he tore off the first page, and he tore off the last page, and he scissored off half of the second-last page.

He said to me, "Look, you warmed up for a page before you started your story and wound down for a page and a half after the story was finished. Don't do that."

I'm not slow to pick up on good advice. I followed Valgardson's instructions, and in one week, during 1975, I sold five stories to magazines, as many as I had sold in the previous five years. And I've sold everything I've written ever since.

The story of Allen Sapp and Dr. Allan Gonor is well known, and has many parallels to my own story. Dr. Gonor recognized Allen's talent, was able to see beyond the calendar art Allen first offered for sale, and had the forthrightness to advise Allen to paint what he knew best — his memories from growing up on the Red Pheasant Reserve.

THE ART OF ALLEN SAPP was like an extension of my own life, for I had as a child watched haying and the cutting of firewood; I had ridden high atop a load of hay, our team of black horses pulling the load across a freshly cut field. In winter, I had ridden over snowy fields beside my father on a load of rails, which would later be cut into firewood, pulled by a horse-drawn sleigh.

My family travelled by horse and sleigh in winter, wrapped in blankets and horse-hide or moose-skin robes, with heated rocks at our feet to keep the frost away. In summer, we made the same journeys by horse and cart, all exposed body parts smeared with citronella to keep mosquitos and black flies at bay.

Allen's paintings brought back the good memories of my childhood, the beauty of the outdoors, the after-rain freshness of the air, the call of birds, the smell of wildflowers.

JUST GETTING HOME   *1985   Acrylic on canvas   60.96 cm x 91.44 cm (24" x 36")   Private collection*

They are just getting home before dark after visiting friends. The children have been playing outside, waiting for their mother and father to return.

WILL HAVE ENOUGH HAY FOR ALL WINTER   *1981   Acrylic on canvas   60.96 cm x 91.44 cm (24" x 36")   Allen Sapp Paintings Inc.*
The hay has been loaded and we are ready to go home. There should be enough to last the winter.

While I am not a qualified art critic, I know when a painting touches my heart, as so many of Allen's do, and when my eyes tear at the perfection of Allen's recollection, the feeling is so special, so personal as to be almost an epiphany.

Allen's paintings present truth as memory edits it. Through them we see and experience the beauty of winter without the bitter cold, without the sensation of biting prairie winds stinging the eyes and bringing instant frostbite to exposed skin. In other words, the outdoors and the elements, while realistically represented, are depicted without the ever-present factors of danger and discomfort, without nature's constant threat to cause suffering.

His memories of summer edit out the torment of black flies and mosquitos. In the indoor scenes, the cabins are spacious, light, swept clean of clutter, perhaps enhanced by the comforting presence of a loved one. The stifling odors of poverty seem to be replaced in memory by the odors of cooking food.

I do much the same in my stories. We each portray the world as a much better, much kinder place than it really is. In my fictions about Indian life, as in Allen Sapp's paintings, the warts have been obliterated, the cracks filled with putty.

In my fiction, I seldom deal with the problems alcohol and drugs bring to Canadian natives, and neither does Allen. He has stated that he is embarrassed to show his people in a negative light.

While it wouldn't embarrass me to use negative material, and I have plenty of negative material I could use — social workers and people who have worked as administrators or taught on reserves are quick to supply me with factual material, much of it of a frightening nature — but I am first and foremost, as a fiction writer always should be, an entertainer. I don't want to shock my readers. *Disturbing* is not an adjective I want applied to my fiction.

I want to present a semblance of reality, but a reality my readers can relate to. I often tell writing students that nine out of ten of us have lives that are boring and uninteresting, so they shouldn't write autobiography. At the same time I point out that the tenth person's life is so bizarre that no one would believe it if it were written down.

The information provided to me by well-meaning individuals with first-hand knowledge of reserve life is generally too bizarre to be presented, even as fiction.

If I repeated the material that has been passed to me, readers would say, "Come on, Kinsella, things can't be that bad. You're making up these stories."

Of course I'm making up my stories, but readers, for whatever reason, want to believe that what they are consciously reading as fiction is true. But that's another essay entirely.

So both Allen Sapp and I present a sanitized version of reality. And I think we are both right and correct to do so.

ANOTHER SIMILARITY, though I'm not certain how much it influences our creative process, is that Allen Sapp and I are both fond of what we regard as beautiful clothes, *beautiful* equating with *bright* in our vocabularies. We both like Western-style clothing, shirts in particular, silks and satins and sashes, and embroidery. And jewellery. I am fond of colourful rings, while Allen likes belt buckles and shiny brooches to decorate the crown of his cowboy hat.

ALTHOUGH I DIDN'T ATTEND any school until grade 5, studying instead by correspondence, with my mother acting as teacher, Allen, as I've mentioned, was forced to attend a white man's residential school at Onion Lake, Saskatchewan.

"I didn't like it," Allen says. "Used to hate it. I get lonesome."

Allen just wanted to draw.

"Oh, I didn't pay attention too much to writing. We supposed to do writing in school.

"The teacher came along one day [when Allen was drawing] and said to me, "'Hey, Allen, what're you doing? You're supposed to be writing. You're a bad boy.'"

The teacher punished him by slapping his hand.

Allen has described himself as illiterate by choice. He'd recognized early in his life that art was his preoccupation — everything else was secondary.

While I was never actually punished for being a writer, I was certainly discouraged from my calling and regarded as a total outsider because I wanted to be a storyteller. In school my only interest was English. I graduated from high school with ninety percent in English and fifty-one percent in each of seven other subjects,

CREE CHIEF   *1971   Acrylic on canvas   50.8 cm x 40.64 cm (20" x 16")   Allen Sapp Paintings Inc.*
A Cree chief looks nice when he has his headdress on. Young people should honour and respect older people, especially the chief.

GOING TO SING A SONG   *1980   Acrylic on canvas   40.64 cm x 50.8 cm (16" x 20")   Allen Sapp Paintings Inc.*
My people like singing and playing the drums. Sometimes I play the drums and sing at home.

Allen Sapp painting outdoors, 1976

which I consciously forgot the instant I finished the last examination in each. I *knew* that I would never have any use for physics, chemistry, algebra, French, or physical education, and I was right — I never have. Just as being illiterate by choice has not stopped Allen Sapp from being one of North America's foremost painters, so confining my interest to reading and writing English has not hampered my career as a writer-storyteller.

Had I received any kind of encouragement to write, I'm sure I could have achieved success at least ten years earlier than I did. But in the 1950s there were no role models for young writers. If one claimed to be a writer or artist, the common reply was "And how long have you been unemployed?"

PHOTO: OWEN EINSIEDLER

Allen Sapp standing in front of the Allen Sapp Gallery —
The Gonor Collection, North Battleford, Saskatchewan, 1989

And though Allen's struggle to survive was considerably more difficult than mine — he spent years on the reserve and later in North Battleford sometimes receiving welfare, sometimes holding menial jobs just to keep food on the table — we each had the resolve and tenacity to continue our artistic endeavours. I wrote occasionally for magazines and newspapers, while writing unsuccessful stories. Allen continued to draw with whatever materials were available to him, using pencil or charcoal and plain paper when nothing else was at hand.

Allen made the first sales of his art when he was in school at Onion Lake. He drew a series of Indian heads, "almost the size of the new dollar, the Loonie. I made quite a few little heads after that, then a white lady gave me five cents. That five cents, brand-new money, makes me happy."

THEY GOT A LOAD OF WOOD   *1989   Acrylic on canvas   60.96 cm x 91.44 cm (24" x 36")   Allen Sapp Paintings Inc.*

Cutting wood in the winter was hard work, but I didn't mind. It was a nice feeling when we had the wagon all loaded up and ready to go.

THE POW-WOW *1987 Acrylic on canvas 101.6 cm x 152.4 cm (40" x 60") Allen Sapp Paintings Inc.*

At a big pow-wow, many people dress in fancy costumes to dance. Drummers and singers are ready. Older people sit and watch.

My first publication was with the *Edmonton Journal* when I was eighteen — a column called "A Tribute to Toys," for which I received a cent a word, for a total of just under seven dollars. I had my first fiction published about the same time — two stories in the *Alberta Civil Service Journal* — "I Walk Through the Valley" and "These Changing Times," fantastical, futuristic fiction; they were not bad stories, coming as they did from a beginning writer.

Today, having carved out successful careers, we each live quietly, shunning most social gatherings, preferring home life to travelling. Allen enjoys attending pow-wows, dressing in one of his colourful costumes and taking part in the ritual dancing. I enjoy making public appearances to read from my work and field questions afterward. But we both shy away from cocktail parties, not just because we are non-drinkers, but because we are uncomfortable in transitory situations.

THE ARTIST
AND THE INSPIRATION

ON JANUARY 2, 1929, Allen Sapp was born to Agnes and Alex Sapp in a little wooden cabin on the Red Pheasant Reserve in northern Saskatchewan.

On May 20, 1923, Allan Gonor was born to Fanny (Penny) and Marcus (Max) Gonor, in Zvenigorodka, U.S.S.R. Only the most imaginative fiction writer could have dreamed that these two individuals, born thousands of miles apart, into cultures remarkably different, would someday be bound together in a relationship so close that they might have been blood brothers.

While the move of Allen Sapp from the reserve to the city of North Battleford, Saskatchewan, was measured not in miles but in change of lifestyle and culture, the move of Allan Gonor was one covering an enormous distance from the Soviet Union to his adopted country, Canada.

When they at last met, as adults, the talent of the natural artist, Allen Sapp, would be inspired to greater heights by the dedicated physician, Allan Gonor, who all his life was genuinely interested in each and every person he met. It seemed destined that these two, Allen Sapp, only recently removed from the reserve, a move that took a great deal of courage and will, and Allan Gonor, recently embarked on a medical career in a small Saskatchewan city, should come together and, through mutual admiration and hard work, see Sapp become one of North America's premier artists.

Nokum Getting Bannock Ready to Cook   *1989   Acrylic on canvas   76.2 cm x 60.96 cm (30" x 24")   Allen Sapp Paintings Inc.*
Grandmother is busy preparing the dough to make bannock.

GOING VISITING *1981 Acrylic on canvas 60.96 cm x 91.44 cm (24" x 36") Allen Sapp Paintings Inc.*

After the work was done, the horses were hitched up to the wagon and the family would start out to visit some friends.

What was it that led a shy young Indian, walking the streets of North Battleford, not yet daring to call himself an artist, but determined to somehow earn money from his natural ability to sketch and paint, into the office of Dr. Allan Gonor, the aspiring young doctor, trying to establish a practice and support his own family?

The story is told that a friend suggested to Allen Sapp that he visit Dr. Gonor, but a misunderstanding ensued and Allen thought the office was located in Saskatoon, some ninety miles away. He wasted a day or two hitchhiking to Saskatoon and fruitlessly searching for the doctor, only to discover that his clinic was only a few blocks away in North Battleford.

When they finally met, Dr. Gonor, though no connoisseur of the arts, sensed instinctively that the paintings Allen showed him were evidence of great talent, mostly hidden. Speaking to Allen, Dr. Gonor was impressed with the dedication of this young man who had left the security of family and reserve life and moved to a strange city in order to become an artist. Allen was a regular sight on the streets of North Battleford, a diffident young man in a suit jacket and horn-rimmed glasses, carrying a package wrapped in brown paper, which contained his few sketches and paintings. He would paint at night, then walk the streets all day to find buyers for his work, even if his prices were low and his income small.

Allen recalls one of his sales: "Sometimes I would draw people. One time a man said to me, 'Would you draw me?' I said, 'Sure.' After I was finished and showed it to him he said, 'That's good,' took out his wallet and gave me two dollars. I was so happy."

He tells about going into the local police station to try to sell a painting.

"Before I entered I thought, Boy, this place looks kind of scary. I'll try anyway. It doesn't hurt to try. So I went in the door. There was a policeman sitting at the desk and he asked me, 'What do you want?'

"'I am Allen Sapp and I want to sell some pictures,' I said.

"'You might get into trouble,' said the policeman.

"'Why should I get into trouble when I'm just trying to help myself?' I replied.

"The police officer then said to me, 'Let me see.'

"I handed him the pictures.

"'How much?'

"'About thirty-five bucks,' I said.

"'Okay, I'll take them.'

"I was so happy that he bought the pictures. I put the money in my pocket and went home."

Some of Allen Sapp's first friends in North Battleford were the Berryman family. Ethel Berryman operated a hobby shop and was very helpful to Allen. She not only supplied him with paints and brushes — sometimes the supplies were gifts — but gave the young Indian fresh from the reserve much-needed encouragement.

ALLEN SAPP REMEMBERS MOST VIVIDLY and paints with such passion scenes from his childhood years during the Great Depression and just prior to the Second World War. The prairies had not been settled that long, and the immigrants coming primarily from Europe were often regarded as intruders by the first settlers who were largely of British descent. The original people, the natives, were mainly confined to reserves and ignored. The great migration to the cities, by both immigrants and natives, had not yet begun. The natives had their own culture and were not as ready as the immigrants to assimilate into the broader culture. The natives were treated paternalistically, and at every level of education and interaction were discouraged from speaking their own languages and preserving their own identities. They were made to feel ashamed for practising their ceremonies, and in many cases those ceremonies, such as the Sun Dance, were banned by government order.

Prior to the mass settlement of the prairies, the whole area was home to many native tribes, including the Cree people, to whom Allen Sapp belongs. During summer, there was much hunting and fishing and preserving of meat and berries for the long winters ahead, when many of the Cree would move to wooded areas, which offered at least some protection from the bitter winter weather. When the Cree people had settled on reserves in response to treaties that had been negotiated with Queen Victoria, some families adjusted their lifestyles and made an attempt at farming.

ESQUOIO HANGING THE MEAT TO DRY IN THE SUN   *1988   Acrylic on canvas   45.72 cm x 60.96 cm (18" x 24")   Allen Sapp Paintings Inc.*
There were different ways to store food when there were no refrigerators. The meat was hung out in the sun to dry and then kept for use later on.

SINGING A SONG   *1972   Acrylic on canvas   45.72 cm x 60.96 cm (18" x 24")   Allen Sapp Paintings Inc.*
The sound of someone playing the drums makes me feel good.

PHOTO: ALEX BALYCH

Allen Sapp outside a log cabin at the Red Pheasant Reserve, 1976

One of those who tried farming, and was successful at it, was Albert Soonias, Allen Sapp's grandfather. Allen proudly speaks of the time "my grandfather had over one hundred head of cattle." Allen's grandmother also kept many chickens, and as a result of his grandparents' success, the whole extended family, including Allen, was able to enjoy a standard of living considerably above that of the average Cree. Eventually, however, inadequate government policies, the jealousy of white settlers, and the overall effects of the Depression forced many Indians, including Allen Sapp, onto welfare.

Alex Sapp, Allen's father, is still alive and living on the Onion Lake Reserve in Saskatchewan. Because Allen's mother died when he was quite young, Maggie Soonias, his grandmother, was the most important and influential person in his life, and Allen speaks of her with great love and reverence. Allen also keeps her alive in memory, as many of his paintings feature her in various poses. It is safe to say that if it had not been for Maggie Soonias, there would not have been Allen Sapp the artist.

While Allen received only condemnation and ridicule from his peers and teachers at school — he would often draw instead of even attempting other lessons — it was his grandmother who gave him the commendation and encouragement that provided the incentive he needed to keep on drawing and later paint.

Allen remembers when he was a little boy, saying to his grandmother, "'Can I draw you?' Grandmother said, 'Okay.' So I drew her.

"My grandmother then said to me, 'You keep on drawing like this. You may be lucky in the future.' Then she told me, 'Don't be a bad boy. Be a good boy and everything will be all right.'"

Allen was an obedient child, and he believed what his grandmother said; he followed her simple admonitions, and her encouragement gave Allen the confidence to continue doing something different.

Allen had many obstacles to overcome as a child. He was puny and underweight and constantly ill. When he was eight years old, Maggie Soonias' elder sister, the Nootokao, or elder, had a dream in which Allen was in imminent danger of dying. It was decided that the Nootokao was to give him a new Indian name, one that would allow him to live long and prosperously. The Nootokao stood by Allen's bedside, touched his forehead, and named him Kiskayetum, He-perceives-it.

In the catalogue for the Allen Sapp Exhibition at the Mendel Gallery in Saskatoon, Rodney Soonias, a cousin of Allen's, talked of Allen's early relationship to the people on the Red Pheasant Reserve. "Allen was always different. He was always liked . . . but you know how it is when a fellow keeps to himself and is sick for a long time. We just thought he'd never make it."

HAULING HAY   *1989   Acrylic on canvas   45.72 cm x 60.96 cm (18" x 24")   Allen Sapp Paintings Inc.*

It took a little while to load up and then haul a big load of hay. This hay fed the horses and cattle in winter.

TAKING HAY INTO THE BARN   *1988   Acrylic on canvas   45.72 cm x 60.96 cm (18" x 24")   Allen Sapp Paintings Inc.*

The horses were ready to be fed, so I had better put some more hay into the barn.

Dr. Gonor elaborated on this aspect of Allen's early life in the 1983 CBC documentary, *Four Prairie Artists*:

> When Allen was a little boy he was at the bottom of the pecking order in the social structure of the reserve. He was rather odd in some ways because he used to like going out into the fields or in different areas of the reserve and just stand and look at things. A lot of people made fun of him and called him a standing post. He used to like just looking at the birds and the trees. Little did we know that at that time he was absorbing everything around the reserve, because very fortunately, Allen has a photographic memory. All the things that he used to see as a child he brings forth in his paintings.

Allen Sapp's early years on the reserve were happy ones, as he was part of a large extended family. Although his actually living with and being raised by his grandmother was necessitated by the death of his mother, it was not unusual in Indian society for grandparents to be active participants in the rearing of young children. Often the whole extended family would live in close proximity, and it was considered quite natural for children to belong to everyone. While life on the reserve was hard in many ways, it was also free from the stress most people encounter in city living. Hunting, fishing, riding horses — everyday activities for Allen and his family — were useful, healthy pursuits. There was no television and radios were scarce, so young people were quite used to providing their own entertainment and making up their own games.

Horses were part of the life of every Indian boy, and Allen has maintained his love of horses over the years, though since living in the city he has less time to ride, he still enjoys, as do many Indian people, dressing in Western clothing. One of Allen's great joys in life is to go shopping for brightly coloured silk and satin Western shirts with fringes and mother-of-pearl buttons.

HE'S TAKING DOUBLE TREES TO FIX THEM   *1989   Acrylic on canvas   45.72 cm x 60.96 cm (18" x 24")   Allen Sapp Paintings Inc.*
When the double trees broke, they would have to be fixed. You might have to walk back to where you could work on them.

COOKING RABBIT ON A STICK   *1989*   *Acrylic on canvas*   *60.96 cm x 76.2 cm (24" x 30")*   *Allen Sapp Paintings Inc.*

When the men worked out in the bush cutting wood, they would hunt a rabbit. They would then build a fire and cook the rabbit on a stick.

GETTING WATER FOR THE HOUSE   *1984   Acrylic on canvas   50.8 cm x 60.96 cm (20" x 24")   Allen Sapp Paintings Inc.*

We had no running water, so my dad took the horses and went to fill up a barrel with water to bring home.

THEY MEET A MAN ON HORSEBACK   *1989   Acrylic on canvas   45.72 cm x 60.96 cm (18" x 24")   Allen Sapp Paintings Inc.*

When people travelled by sleigh in the winter they would often meet someone on horseback and talk.

DANCING IN THE POW-WOW   *1989   Acrylic on canvas   40.64 cm x 50.8 cm (16" x 20")   Allen Sapp Paintings Inc.*

I always like dressing up in a fancy costume and dancing at the pow-wow. It is a good feeling.

LITTLE BOY PLAYING WITH PUPPY   *1981   Acrylic on canvas   45.72 cm x 60.96 cm (18" x 24")   Allen Sapp Paintings Inc.*

It always seemed that there were puppies around. Little boys especially liked playing with them.

KIDS PLAYING OUTSIDE   *1987   Acrylic on canvas   30.48 cm x 40.64 cm (12" x 16")   Private collection*
It is lots of fun for children to play outside in the snow. They take turns pulling one another on the sleigh.

IT'S NOT A BAD DAY TO WORK   *1988   Acrylic on canvas   60.96 cm x 91.44 cm (24" x 36")   Allen Sapp Paintings Inc.*
The sun is shining and it's a nice winter day. When you are working hard cutting wood you don't get too cold.

A BIG POW-WOW   1988   *Acrylic on canvas   60.96 cm x 91.44 cm (24" x 36")   Allen Sapp Paintings Inc.*

The dancers are ready for the grand entry. The pow-wow is ready to begin.

WAITING FOR THE TRAIN AT RED PHEASANT RESERVE   *1989   Acrylic on canvas   60.96 cm x 91.44 cm (24" x 36")   Allen Sapp Paintings Inc.*

It was cold when we were waiting for the train. One time I remember going to Prince Albert. It seemed like such a long trip.

PEOPLE JUST GOT HOME   *1982   Acrylic on canvas   45.72 cm x 60.96 cm (18" x 24")   Allen Sapp Paintings Inc.*

We liked to go visiting friends, and often we would get home just before dark. In the winter the sky would have many beautiful colours.

HAVING DINNER   *1976   Acrylic on canvas   60.96 cm x 91.44 cm (24" x 36")   Allen Sapp Paintings Inc.*
The old stove was used to cook the dinner and also to keep warm. Some people were so poor that they would eat their meals off the floor.

STRETCHING MOOSE HIDE   *1970   Acrylic on canvas   60.96 cm x 91.44 cm (24" x 36")   Allen Sapp Paintings Inc.*

My grandmother had many talents. She could stretch moose hide and it would then be used to make things.

TEACHING LI'L KIDS *1989 Acrylic on canvas 45.72 cm x 60.96 cm (18" x 24") Allen Sapp Paintings Inc.*
The little kids liked to play outside on the ice soon after they could walk. There was always some older person who taught them how to skate and play hockey.

GOING TO VISIT FRIENDS   *1971   Acrylic on canvas   60.96 cm x 91.44 cm (24" x 36")   Allen Sapp Gallery — The Gonor Collection*
It felt so good riding along in the sleigh over the newly fallen snow. Very peaceful and quiet.

PASSING AROUND THE TEA   *1984   Acrylic on canvas   60.96 cm x 91.44 cm (24" x 36")   Allen Sapp Paintings Inc.*

This is an occasion when we remember someone. We pass around the tea as part of the ceremony.

PRETTY SOON GOING TO BE DARK   *1977   Acrylic on canvas   60.96 cm x 91.44 cm (24" x 36")   Allen Sapp Paintings Inc.*
The man has just come home and he will take his horse into the barn to be fed and watered.

BOYS PLAYING FOOTBALL   *1988   Acrylic on canvas   76.2 cm x 101.6 cm (30" x 40")   Allen Sapp Paintings Inc.*
In the wintertime if there was no ice close to play hockey, the young boys still liked to play outside. They would get something to kick around and play football.

GOING TO VISIT SOME PEOPLE   *1971   Acrylic on canvas   60.96 cm x 91.44 cm (24" x 36")   Allen Sapp Paintings Inc.*

When we went visiting in the winter, the sleigh was the only way to go. There was straw in the sleigh to help keep warm.

BIG BOYS PLAYING HOCKEY   *1988   Acrylic on canvas   60.96 cm x 91.44 cm (24" x 36")   Private Collection*

In the wintertime the boys liked to play hockey wherever they could find some ice. They would have a lot of fun together.

TWO MEN VISITING   *1989   Acrylic on canvas   60.96 cm x 76.2 cm (24" x 30")   Allen Sapp Paintings Inc.*

People nowadays always seem to be in a hurry. It's nice when two men sit down and just talk.

RECESS AT SCHOOL   *1988   Acrylic on canvas   40.64 cm x 50.8 cm (16" x 20")   Allen Sapp Paintings Inc.*

It seemed that one of the nicest things about going to school was recess. Then the children could go outside and play different games.

COOKING SUPPER   *1985   Acrylic on canvas   40.64 cm x 50.8 cm (16" x 20")   Allen Sapp Paintings Inc.*

Supper was often cooked outside in the summer over an open fire. Today people call it barbecuing.

CLEANING THE BARN   *1989   Acrylic on canvas   60.96 cm x 76.2 cm (24" x 30")   Allen Sapp Paintings Inc.*
In the winter the horses were kept in the barn. Someone always had to work and make sure the barn was clean.

PUTTING ON HIS SPURS   1975   *Acrylic on canvas   60.96 cm x 76.2 cm (24" x 30")   Allen Sapp Paintings Inc.*
I like wearing Western clothes — cowboy hats and cowboy boots. I also like rodeos — chuckwagon races and bronco riders.

GOING INTO THE POW-WOW   *1988   Acrylic on canvas   50.8 cm x 60.96 cm (20" x 24")   Private Collection*
Sometimes there was a small pow-wow in the wintertime. The people came on their sleighs and gathered inside.

NOKUM MENDING A BLANKET   *1988   Acrylic on canvas   45.72 cm x 60.96 cm (18" x 24")   Allen Sapp Paintings Inc.*

My grandmother always seemed to be busy doing something. She was good at mending blankets and making quilts.

KIDS HAVING FUN   *1978   Acrylic on canvas   60.96 cm x 76.2 cm (24" x 30")   Allen Sapp Paintings Inc.*

Most of the homes were not very big, so the children spent their time playing outside.

LITTLE BOY WAVING TO FRIENDS   *1982   Acrylic on canvas   60.96 cm x 76.2 cm (24" x 30")   Allen Sapp Paintings Inc.*

Little children always liked to go along on the wagon.

ESQUOIO MAKING BANNOCK   *1986   Acrylic on canvas   45.72 cm x 60.96 cm (18" x 24")   Allen Sapp Paintings Inc.*
In the summertime when the family went to pow-wows, Esquoio made the bannock outside on an open fire. Everyone enjoyed eating the bannock.

GOING TO A CHRISTMAS CONCERT   *1983*   *Acrylic on canvas*   *60.96 cm x 91.44 cm (24" x 36")*   *Allen Sapp Paintings Inc.*
The horse and sleigh would be made ready and then the family went to town for a Christmas concert. The children liked to go, for they always got a little treat.

THE ROUND DANCE   *1987   Acrylic on canvas   101.6 cm x 152.4 cm (40" x 60")   Allen Sapp Paintings Inc.*
The drummers and the singers were very important at a round dance. Everyone is happy to listen to them.

WILL GO INTO THE HOUSE SOON   *1981   Acrylic on canvas   60.96 cm x 91.44 cm (24" x 36")   Allen Sapp Paintings Inc.*
The drums would be heated outside so that they would sound better. The drummers would then go into the house for the round dance.

A letter, first published in 1977 in *A Cree Life: The Art of Allen Sapp*, illustrates what life was like during Allen's formative years.

> When Allen's grandpa died, Allen kept with his grandma in the old log shack. The grandma sold the cattle. But Allen kept the horses and chickens. Allen didn't have no income; he used to take wood to Cando, which is our home town, twelve miles from the reserve. I knew he sold pictures in Cando for $5.00 apiece, sometimes $4.00. But he was shy when he carried them in the streets. And I knew when he used to go to the butcher shop and ask for scraps. In fact, many times he went to the dump grounds. He used to get something outta there. . . . He used to sell wood for $5.00 a load. Many times 40 below zero, he had hard times. The same time he would snare rabbits. Also he used to cut willow pickets and sharpen them. We use to sell them pickets for 3 cents apiece. But mostly we traded it for food. Today Allen laughs and tells of those days without sorrow. . . .

Allan Gonor came to Canada when he was one year old and spent his childhood in Winnipeg. His Jewish family had to face many hardships in Russia, and had to fight an uphill battle as new immigrants in Canada. When Allan was a child, his family was very poor, and the necessities of life were often difficult to come by.

Because of his own first-hand experiences with poverty, it was easy for Allan Gonor to sympathize with Allen Sapp, for their backgrounds were similar in many ways. Ruth Gonor, his widow, mentions that for a long time it was difficult for Sapp to understand why Gonor, a man who in Sapp's eyes was rich and successful, would be interested in him. Yet as time passed, Allen Sapp realized that the friendship extended to him was genuine, and that the friendship with Allan Gonor and his entire family would endure.

The Sapp-Gonor relationship, like all lasting and happy friendships, was based on trust and understanding.

"They were very comfortable with each other," Ruth Gonor recalls. "There was complete trust between them, and they had great respect for one another."

Dr. Allan Gonor, Ruth Gonor, and Allen Sapp in the Gonor living room, 1975

Allan Gonor was what would be described as a Type A personality. He lived as if he were late for an important appointment. In contrast, Allen Sapp does not like to be rushed. Allen likes to flow with the elements; he eats when he is hungry, sleeps when he is tired, and does not like to have to keep regular hours or appointments.

"Dr. Gonor was always in a hurry," Allen Sapp has commented many times.

But in their long relationship, both were able to compromise, and the differences in their personalities and pace at which they lived their lives never became problems.

WARMING THE DRUMS AT THE ROUND DANCE   *1988   Acrylic on canvas   60.96 cm x 91.44 cm (24" x 36")   Allen Sapp Paintings Inc.*
People are ready to go into the round dance. Meanwhile, the drummers are warming their drums outside so that they will sound better.

GETTING THE BIG FENCE FIXED *1986* *Acrylic on canvas* *60.96 cm x 91.44 cm (24" x 36")* *Allen Sapp Paintings Inc.*

One of the things that kept us busy was fixing the fence so the cattle and horses would not be able to get out.

Allan Gonor in his RCAF uniform, 1942

At an exhibition of Sapp's paintings, Allan Gonor would be busy snapping photographs, the movie camera and tape recorder at the ready. His subject was almost always Allen Sapp; consequently, there are countless invaluable photos, movies, and recordings documenting Sapp's career and life, material that might never have existed if it hadn't been for Dr. Gonor's enthusiasm and zeal. Allen Sapp learned well from Dr. Gonor, for he now carries a tape recorder, and tapes all his important conversations for posterity.

Prior to the onset of the Second World War, Allan Gonor worked at a number of menial jobs, such as packing-plant labourer, in the Winnipeg area. His future did not look bright. Taking the advice of a friend, he joined the RCAF — the pay was good and he hoped to become part of a flying crew, perhaps even a pilot. Allan and his friend planned to join up together, but the friend's eyesight did not meet RCAF standards, so the two separated. The friend joined the army, which was less particular about vision, and soon became a sergeant, while Allan Gonor became an officer in the air force. He was a member of the Pathfinder Force serving overseas with the RCAF.

Allan Gonor was happy in the RCAF; his standard of living went up immeasurably, and for the first time he was not enduring poverty. He served as a navigator and saw action during two tours of duty over Europe with the Pathfinders. He was awarded the Distinguished Flying Cross, but was never one to discuss or relive his war exploits. His first-hand view of suffering and the ravages of war did make him more sensitive and compassionate, more interested in his fellow man. Even before he met Allen Sapp, Allan Gonor was greatly moved by the plight of many native people on the reserves in Canada.

Allan Gonor was justly proud to receive the Distinguished Flying Cross, and on his return to Winnipeg speculated that there might be a quite a few people at the station to greet the returning hero. To his amazement, there was only one person he knew at the railway station, a neighbour of his family's. The neighbour was not there to met him; the man in fact did not even know he had been away.

After the war, Allan Gonor discovered that there were government programs for veterans that made it possible for him to further his education. He first spent about a year and a half finishing his senior matriculation. Because of the veterans' programs, Allan realized he could enter almost any profession he wished. His first choice was to become a chartered accountant, but even though his high school marks were high, he was not able to get into that faculty at university. Allen felt that he could compete at any level of learning and after one year of pre-med was accepted into medical school.

Ruth and Allan Gonor met while Allan was taking his senior matriculation.

"It was a sort of an on-and-off affair," Ruth remembers. "I celebrated with him when he got accepted into medical school. When he was in third-year medicine, we were married in Winnipeg. Our honeymoon consisted of a short bus trip."

The Gonors lived in Winnipeg for three more years while Allan completed his medical training. They then moved to Saskatoon, where Allan interned at St. Paul's Hospital. They moved to North Battleford in 1952, where Allan set up practice, and fourteen years later, in 1966, he met Allen Sapp.

Was it the memory of his grandmother saying, "Allen, you keep on drawing . . . You may be lucky in the future," that planted the seeds of determination in the young Allen Sapp, that gave him the courage to uproot himself, travel to a strange city, and risk ridicule to sell his drawings? Was it the constant love and encouragement of Maggie Soonias that gave Allen the desire to improve his lot in life?

Whatever the motives, it was Allen's visit to Dr. Gonor's clinic in North Battleford that was the beginning of a unique partnership that changed both their lives for the better.

In *Four Prairie Artists*, Dr. Gonor described how his relationship with Allen Sapp began:

> I remember seeing Allen Sapp going along the streets of North Battleford carrying a bundle of paintings. I used to buy the odd painting from him, and they were sort of a mixture of calender art featuring moose and mountains, which he had never seen. He used to charge $5, $10, $15, or $20, and I wasn't too excited. The kind of painting I really wanted was of reserve life. When Allen came to our clinic one day trying to sell me some paintings, I told him I would like him to paint me a scene of the reserve as I had seen it, and as Allen knew it.

CHILDREN HAVING FUN   *1986   Acrylic on canvas   60.96 cm x 76.2 cm (24" x 30")   Allen Sapp Paintings Inc.*
The winter is a good time for children to have fun. Their dogs like playing with them in the snow.

READY TO GO HOME NOW   *1981   Acrylic on canvas   50.8 cm x 60.96 cm (20" x 24")   Allen Sapp Paintings Inc.*
The barrel has been filled with water, and after the horses have had a drink we will be heading for home.

He wanted some money in advance as he didn't have enough to buy a proper-size canvas. I gave him some money and he bought a canvas board and some paint, and the next day he came back to see me. He has this beautiful painting of a farmyard scene, which I liked very much. I was very excited and told him I would like to get some more. That was the start of our relationship.

Ruth Gonor recalls that her husband was very enthusiastic when he received Allen Sapp's first paintings of reserve life. Here was a man who was a medical doctor, not a connoisseur of the arts, yet he felt that there was much more to this young native's work than anyone suspected. Allan Gonor had been raised in a working-class home and had no exposure to the arts, so when he decided that Allen Sapp's talent was worth nourishing and promoting, he was responding to his good instincts rather than as a person with a formal arts education.

It was Allan Gonor's innate curiosity, his manic energy, and genuine interest in everyone he met, especially native people, that let to his initially establishing a relationship with Allen Sapp. Over the years Allan Gonor's compassion and curiosity about the native peoples of the world would lead him to the far corners of the earth — Tibet, Antarctica, the Falkland Islands, the Amazon, and China, not once but many times. Dr. Gonor often donated his medical expertise to indigenous peoples all over the world.

When the Gonors moved to North Battleford, Allan Gonor was keen to learn all he could about local native people, their history, their culture. In his medical practice he ministered to many native people, and his association with Allen Sapp gave him the opportunity to learn about and become friends with native people within hundreds of miles of North Battleford.

After Allen Sapp had sold a number of paintings to Allan Gonor, he was invited to visit the doctor at his home. Allen Sapp recalls, "We got along right away. Dr. Gonor was always so happy — he was smiling — and so was his wife."

Dr. Gonor encouraged Allen to paint pictures of life on the reserve as he remembered it. He told Allen Sapp that he would buy his paintings and arrange for the sale of others so that Allen could get off welfare and make a living as an

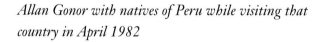

Allan Gonor with natives of Peru while visiting that country in April 1982

artist. This was not an easy decision for Allen; he was reluctant to give up the relative security of monthly welfare, and it took a great deal of reassurance from Dr. Gonor and his family before Allen was finally convinced that the move was a good one.

As it happened, the artist never looked back, and the arrangement proved to be a very rewarding one for him, for it freed him of financial worries while allowing him to spend all his time doing what he loved best, painting. There is no question that this newfound independence, which enabled Allen to think of nothing but painting, made him a better artist.

I'M SETTING A SNARE FOR A RABBIT   *1989   Acrylic on canvas   60.96 cm x 45.72 cm (24" x 18")   Allen Sapp Paintings Inc.*

My dad went out in the bush to set a snare for the rabbits. The next day we would have some rabbit stew.

MY DAD'S HORSES   *1989   Acrylic on canvas   45.72 cm x 60.96 cm (18" x 24")   Allen Sapp Paintings Inc.*
Before the cars came along everyone had horses. My dad had a good team and really liked working with them.

Almost involuntarily, the entire Gonor family became engaged as the Gonor-Sapp relationship became more intense. Sons Saul and David would stretch the canvases on which Allen painted. As Allen became more comfortable with the whole Gonor family, he felt free to visit them at any time.

Ruth Gonor recalls that Allen, who has always painted at night, would often phone very late, sometimes long after midnight, immediately after finishing a new painting. When Ruth answered the phone, Allen would say, "It's late, I shouldn't be calling you." However, Ruth would reassure him, and he would respond with pleasure when she invited him to come right over. Allen would arrive at the Gonor residence in a few moments, bearing the new painting.

There would follow a cup of hot tea and some fresh baking, which Ruth always had handy. After a snack and a short visit, Allen would return home. He was like a member of the Gonor household.

Although Allen no longer delivers his paintings to the Gonor home in the middle of the night, he is still a frequent visitor, and is always welcomed by Ruth Gonor with the offer of a cup of tea, a piece of pie, or a light lunch.

ALLAN GONOR ARRANGED for Wynona Mulcaster, an art professor at the University of Saskatchewan in Saskatoon who is widely respected for her ardent support of native art, to become Allen's adviser. During the winter of 1967, Allan Gonor drove Allen Sapp to Saskatoon every Saturday so he could meet with Mulcaster. She encouraged Allen to paint the Indian way of life: "You must paint the way your people feel, paint the experiences you have had as an Indian." (It was a great tribute to Allen Sapp that at the opening and dedication of the Allen Sapp Gallery — The Gonor Collection in 1989 in the fully renovated old library building in North Battleford, Wynona Mulcaster was the keynote speaker. Her text is included in this book.)

As Allen Sapp's paintings became popular, it was necessary to arrange gallery showings and public appearances to promote his work. What had started as one man's helping another to make a living at his chosen craft had now become a business, and Dr. Gonor was too busy to continue guiding all aspects of Allen's career, so a business manager, Bill Baker, was retained. Although Baker lived and worked in Vancouver, there were lengthy consultations by phone involving Dr. Gonor and Allen Sapp about subject matter, exhibitions, and appearances.

OFTEN ALLEN WILL PAINT from unusual perspectives, as in the painting *Dancing in the Pow-Wow*, (page 45) or *Going to Visit Friends*, (page 55). Dr. Gonor talked about this aspect of Allen's work in the 1973 National Film Board production *The Colours of Pride*, an excellent film on native artists Norval Morrisseau, Daphne Odjig, Alex Janvier, and Allen Sapp:

> A lot of the things he is painting are things he remembers as a youngster. I remember there are some paintings depicting the inside of a cabin, and in the front part of the painting the legs of the table are a bit high. I asked Allen how come, as it looks a bit out of proportion, and Allen said he was just a little boy lying on the floor, and it sure looked awfully big at the time.

In the same vein are the paintings from the perspective of a bedridden person, as Allen had been during his bout of meningitis.

Allen's paintings are a chronicle of life on the plains, outdoors in the summer, hauling hay and water and some indoor scenes in winter, playing, eating, baking bannock, as well as the ever-present outdoor chores of cutting and hauling wood, and travelling to visit family and friends.

In another CBC documentary, *By Instinct a Painter*, made in 1971 for the "Telescope" series, Wynona Mulcaster talked of Allen Sapp's amazing recall:

> I went with him to visit the old cabin where he was brought up with his grandparents. Here the logs remain of what was once their dwelling. We stepped in through the open doorway, and Allen stood in this cabin and pointed out to me, 'Here, this is where the stove used to be, this is where the woodpile was. Here's the window my grandmother used to sit beside when she was peeling potatoes. And my grandmother slept over here, and I slept over here,' and so on. And I could just see it. He had painted so many paintings of this same house, and his memory was so complete, I'm sure even the

YOUNG MOTHER AND BABY   *1984   Acrylic on canvas   40.64 cm x 50.8 cm (16" x 20")   Allen Sapp Paintings Inc.*
Little babies should be loved and looked after. My grandmother looked after me when I was young.

GRANDMOTHER DRINKING SOME TEA   *1976   Acrylic on canvas   45.72 cm x 60.96 cm (18" x 24")   Allen Sapp Paintings Inc.*

My grandmother liked sitting by the stove drinking tea. She would think about many things that had happened.

PHOTO: ALEX BALYCH

Allen in traditional dancing attire, 1977

number of logs was correct. And I could just stand in the doorway and see his grandmother there, and I could see the woodpile. I could see the stove because I had seen it in paintings before. So from this vivid memory all his experiences as a boy must have been tremendously important, very vital to him. He recalls each of them with amazing clarity. There is no pretence. When you look at these paintings and you know a little bit about the Indian life and the Indian way of living, they are right.

There are several works that illustrate the interior of Allen's home. Included are *Suppertime*, (page 97), and *Little Boy Playing with Puppy*, (page 46).

ALTHOUGH MANY NATIVE CULTURAL PRACTICES were at one time criticized by society and banned by government, native culture did not die but simply went underground. Rather than lamenting the past, the native people today proudly participate in these events. Allan Sapp affirms that much of his inspiration and enthusiasm for painting comes after he has renewed himself by participating in the once-frowned-on rituals of pow-wows and Sun Dances. Allen is an accomplished dancer and likes to dance at pow-wows while dressed in colourful regalia. Once, a visitor from Germany inquired of Dr. Gonor where he might find Allen Sapp, to which Dr. Gonor replied, "Allen Sapp the artist?" "No," answered the visitor, "Allen Sapp the dancer."

An Indian pow-wow is a happy occasion, which also has a spiritual side to it. Indian people will travel long distances to attend pow-wows. The dancers, young and old, men and women, wear beautiful costumes and often perform in a variety of dances and dance competitions. Soon after the two men met, Dr. Gonor was invited to a pow-wow as Allen Sapp's guest. Dr. Gonor was enthralled by the pageantry of the pow-wows and attended many more over the years, always photographing, photographing. He was loved and trusted by the native people and was sometimes allowed to film and photograph ceremonies that no white man had even been allowed to attend.

Bob Boyer, head of the Department of Indian Fine Arts, Saskatchewan Indian Federated College, University of Regina, and a friend of Allen Sapp's, has this to say about pow-wows:

PHOTO: McINTOSH PUBLISHING

Allen Sapp and Allan Gonor at the North Battleford Pow-wow, 1974

The modern-day pow-wow developed in the Plains Indian cultures over the centuries. Its roots can be directly traced to the Omaha or Grass Dance Societies of Nebraska and Oklahoma in the 1800s.

Initially the Omaha Societies followed very prescribed dances, ceremonies, and feasts in order to celebrate and entertain in their respective communities. This, however, changed with the advent of the reservation life and the twentieth century. The Grass Dance Society, once only one of many societies to bring social life to the communities, gradually became more important as a cultural focal point. As other societies on the plains were let go, the pow-wow societies grew stronger and larger. They grew to a point where, today, they may be at times the largest expression of Plains Indian music, dance, art, prayer, and ceremony.

NEEDS WATER FOR THE HOME   *1978   Acrylic on canvas   60.96 cm x 45.72 cm (24" x 18")   Allen Sapp Paintings Inc.*

Some people would be lucky and have a well close by. They were able to get water in a pail and walk home with it.

SUMMER POW-WOW AT PIAPOT   *1987   Acrylic on canvas   60.96 cm x 91.44 cm (24" x 36")   Private collection*

I meet many friends and I feel really happy when I am dancing at pow-wows.

Today, at a pow-wow, spectators may witness Plains Indian dancing, music, art, prayer, and ceremony all under one roof. The modern-day pow-wow is a centre for Plains Indian culture, and in that sense must be deemed invaluable to the preservation of the arts and spirituality in the Indian community. The pow-wow is accessible to the general public to view and participate in at whatever level they are prepared. At these modern-day spectacles, you will witness the young and old dancing and celebrating together. The young will learn from the old, and the old will for a time regain their youth. The pow-wow is still strong and it is still growing.

It is to this Pow-wow Society that Allen Sapp belongs. He is a dancer who has grown up with the dances, the songs, the ceremonies, and the prayers. He knows these things, and when he paints these things they are correct.

ALLEN SAPP AND ALLAN GONOR SHARED a lively sense of humour, never taking themselves too seriously. On one occasion, the late Irwin McIntosh, then lieutenant governor of Saskatchewan and a native of North Battleford, invited Allen Sapp, Dr. Gonor, and some friends to dinner in Regina. Although Allen Sapp was never too excited about fancy or high-class affairs, as he calls them, he accepted the invitation because he felt it was necessary not to offend important people as he was soon to have a showing of his paintings at the Assiniboia Gallery in Regina.

After a sumptuous meal and a good deal of conversation, Allen yawned and said, "I feel real tired. Think maybe I will excuse myself and go back to the hotel."

"I believe I'll go with Allen," Dr. Gonor said, and expressed his regrets at leaving the lieutenant governor.

Irwin McIntosh was quite amused when he learned sometime later that Allen and Dr. Gonor had gone to a Western movie, Allen Sapp's favourite kind, and not back to their hotel.

Allen still prefers a lifestyle not unlike his humble beginnings, and the grand circumstances he sometimes finds himself in provide opportunities for his playful irony. After opening an exhibition at La Galerie Continental in Montreal, Allen was invited to dinner at an exclusive restaurant. When the waiter in these opulent

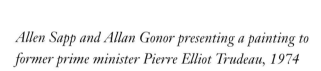

Allen Sapp and Allan Gonor presenting a painting to former prime minister Pierre Elliot Trudeau, 1974

surroundings asked what he would like, Allen's reply was "How about some rabbit stew?" To his surprise, the restaurant had rabbit meat on the menu.

However, Allen settled for a steak, adding, "Rabbit tastes better roasted outside."

He recalls his father's shooting a rabbit, skinning it in the bush in winter, then saying, "Now we can eat. I've brought along some bannock, some tea — we'll make a fire and have lunch."

Allen remarks that the white man now calls this barbecuing.

Although he doesn't do any hunting himself, he has friends who hunt and bring him rabbit and deer meat. He continues to feel that cooking meat outdoors is the best method.

STARTING ANOTHER LOAD   *1986   Acrylic on canvas   60.96 cm x 76.2 cm (24" x 30")   Allen Sapp Paintings Inc.*

There was always lots of wood to cut in the winter. This was a good way to make a few dollars to buy food for the family.

SUPPERTIME   *1979   Acrylic on canvas   40.64 cm x 50.8 cm (16" x 20")   Allen Sapp Paintings Inc.*

The family is seated at the table ready for supper. Before the mother will eat, she will make sure that the baby is fed.

Allan Gonor at the Falkland Islands in December 1981

While visiting Montreal recently, Allen hailed a taxi and asked to be taken to a specific store that sells Western clothing. The taxi driver, apparently not understanding, drove Allen to a different store, where he, good-natured as always, said, "Let's go in anyway."

When he walked into Kellams of Montreal Ltd. on St. Catherine Street, he was greeted by Elias Dabby, who exclaimed, "My friend, where have you been? It has been many years since you were last in my store!" Allen immediately recognized Mr. Dabby and they exchanged warm greetings. The occasion turned out to be a happy one, for Allen was able to buy some of the fanciest Western shirts and cowboy boots he had seen in some time.

Allen was in such good spirits after visiting the Western store that while riding a taxi to the airport to catch his flight back to Regina, he asked the cab driver if it would be all right if he sang. There, driving down St. Catherine Street in a taxi, Allen sang in Cree to the cab driver, accompanied by the beat of an imaginary drum.

DR. GONOR BECAME ACTIVELY INTERESTED in people of the world, and in travelling, about the same time as he discovered Allen Sapp. In his travels, he met many influential people, and he always managed to tell the story of the Cree artist he was championing. If Dr. Gonor could not accomplish something himself, he would always find someone of his acquaintance who could provide whatever was needed to advance the career of Allen Sapp.

It was the director of the Winnipeg Art Gallery, Dr. Ferdinand Eckhardt, who suggested to Dr. Gonor that Wynona Mulcaster might be able to help Allen Sapp. It was she who sponsored the first exhibition of Sapp's paintings, an informal showing at her own home. The exhibition was a huge success, and if there was one event that was pivotal in launching the career of Allen Sapp as a major Canadian artist, that was it.

In 1967 Ruth and Allan Gonor visited Montreal in an effort to excite interest in Allen Sapp's paintings. A Montreal art dealer at the Eaton's gallery was impressed enough that he exhibited Allen's paintings in March 1968. Again, thanks to Dr. Gonor's untiring efforts, that exhibition gained for Allen the attention of discriminating art buyers in Montreal, and the recognition he received there provided a springboard for national and international attention. There have been many exhibitions in Montreal over the years, and those showings have been attended by many Sapp collectors from New York City.

In 1969, 13,000 people viewed an exhibition of Allen Sapp's paintings at the Mendel Art Gallery, in Saskatoon, Saskatchewan. The number of viewers was extremely impressive, as were the sales of almost sixty of Allen's paintings. There are many astute collectors of art in Saskatoon, and the Mendel Gallery occupies an important place in the Canadian art world, (on a per capita basis, the attendance at the Mendel Art Gallery is second only to that of the National Gallery in Ottawa); thus the recognition of Allen Sapp's work at that exhibition was a giant step forward for his career.

Additional exhibitions were held in London, England, and in New York and Los Angeles. Suddenly the paintings of Allen Sapp became part of many important collections. During this period, Dr. Gonor met Will and Ariel Durant, noted historians and authors of *The Story of Civilization*. Will Durant was very impressed with the painting of this native Canadian artist, stating that there is almost a European feeling or influence in his art. Will Durant described Allen Sapp as "one of the healthiest and finest painters of our time."

Zachery Waller, owner of the Zachery Waller Gallery in Los Angeles, said of Allen Sapp's work:

> The more that Allen digs into what he is and records the life that was his and was handed down to him, the more he will be able to record a whole era of life which will only be remembered because he has taken the time to paint it.

Victor Hammer wrote in the catalogue for the Allen Sapp exhibition at the Hammer Galleries in New York in 1976:

> In a forthright statement he transmits the emotion of the Crees' acceptance of their environment. In the lonely landscape there is a solidarity of purpose and the chores are accomplished despite the elements, and life continues immutably. There is a challenging integrity in the paintings that transcends realism.

NOKUM LOOKING AFTER THE CHICKENS   *1989   Acrylic on canvas   60.96 cm x 45.72 cm (24" x 18")   Allen Sapp Paintings Inc.*
Nokum had lots of chickens and always made sure they had enough to eat. Sometimes I would go into the henhouse and gather eggs.

HOLDING HER BABY   *1980   Acrylic on canvas   45.72 cm x 60.96 cm (18" x 24")   Allen Sapp Paintings Inc.*
It will soon be time for the baby to go to sleep. The mother is holding her until she settles down.

"Internationally recognized Pulitzer Prize winning author and historian, Will Durant, with daughter Ethel, is shown accepting an original painting by Allen Sapp from Dr. Allan Gonor on the occasion of Durant's 90th birthday. This event also coincided with the publication of the book The Age of Napoleon, *the 11th volume in the formidable series* The Story of Civilization, *authored by Durant and his wife Ariel."*
– North Battleford News-Optimist
February 27, 1976

Today, Allen has exhibitions in all the major cities of Canada — Victoria, Vancouver, Edmonton, Calgary, Regina, Saskatoon, Winnipeg, Toronto, Ottawa, Montreal. Until 1976, when the Assiniboia Gallery began showing the works of Allen Sapp in Regina, many Regina residents travelled all the way to Toronto to purchase Sapp's paintings.

Many fans have written to Allen Sapp expressing their appreciation of his paintings and trying to convey what those paintings mean to them. The following letter is an example of the deep emotion Sapp's paintings arouse in people.

Vancouver, B.C. — (Dec. 15/88 - Nov. 1/89)

Dear Mr. Sapp,

I began writing this letter almost a year ago! I wanted to tell you that one of your paintings has found me. I first heard of you in Oct./88. I was visiting the home of Nancy Morrison. She is from Saskatchewan and has two of your paintings. Then, two weeks later, an article about you in a local magazine. Then, again, two weeks later I walked into a gallery around the corner from my office, and saw *Just Passing Through*. Immediately I felt drawn to this painting. I love the sky, the shadows on the snow, and especially the child bundled in the beautiful blanket riding on the sleigh.

I am a musician, songwriter and singer. It is a magical and special feeling to know you have touched someone with your expression of your reality. I wanted to tell you that *Just Passing Through* is a song for me, a song of color, emotion, and feelings. It is the first work of art I have purchased, and I am glad it is one of yours. It is like a friend to me. It hangs on a wall facing east in my little apartment, the light plays on it so exquisitely! It has a cozy mood about it, and a stillness too.

I hope I have the opportunity to meet you and thank you personally. Your artistry and honesty is much appreciated.

Sincerely,
Devon Hanley

IT IS FASCINATING to see the reactions of art critics to Allen Sapp's work. Diana Loercher, of the *Christian Science Monitor* (May 5, 1976), wrote:

There is in his paintings an atmosphere of stillness and timelessness and sensitivity to the nuances of nature — the texture of grass, the changes of the seasons, the shades of the sky — all rendered in an almost Scandinavian palate of brown, blue and white flecked with color. Mr. Sapp has great reverence for the land, a tradition in Indian religion, and derives much of his inspiration from nature. A radiant light permeates most of his paintings because of his worship of the sun which "shines down on a cloud and gives light so that people can see."

My Grandfather Had So Many Cows   *1987*   *Acrylic on canvas*   *91.44 cm x 60.96 cm (36" x 24")*   *Allen Sapp Paintings Inc.*

There was a time when my grandfather had over one hundred head of cattle. There was enough for everyone and also some to sell to other people.

HE IS GOING HOME   *1971   Acrylic on canvas   60.96 cm x 91.44 cm (24" x 36")   Allen Sapp Gallery — The Gonor Collection*
It's been a long day and it took quite a while to load the wagon with hay. It is time to go home.

Marjorie Earl, writing in the *Winnipeg Tribune* (November 8, 1977):

> In his art Sapp seems almost haunted by one of the absolute wonders of the prairie landscape, the long winter blue twilight. Many of his paintings are soft, muted and overcast with this beautiful but eerie light.

Meta Perry, writing in the *Regina Leader Post* (November 14, 1985), talked about a Sapp winter painting, *They Have Visitors*, painted in 1985.

> Two horses stand in front of a cabin against a background of frost-covered trees. It is sunset, and it is cold, as the blue shadows in the sky and on the snow suggest. In the painting, varied brush strokes and thickly applied paint create texture. The snow, for example, is created by thick swirls of paint that look like piled and drifted snow.
>
> In some places, the paint actually stands out from the canvas. The logs of the cabin are thick bands of paint. Short, feathery brush strokes make the frosty trees, evenly applied yellow paint is used for the sky.

At an exhibition in a Toronto gallery, an art professor was heard to remark, "He does all the right things, but he doesn't know why he does them." She went on to explain that here was an artist with no formal training, a self-taught artist, who, being "by instinct a painter," was able to accomplish marvellous work on canvas, using techniques worthy of the most highly trained artist.

During the early years of the Gonor-Sapp relationship, as acceptance of Allen Sapp's paintings grew, the Gonor home in North Battleford became the unofficial gallery for Allen Sapp paintings. Visitors from Canada, the United States, and Europe were graciously welcomed by the Gonors to examine their huge collection of Sapp paintings and to view the many home movies, photographs, television documentaries, articles, and press clippings Dr. Gonor had so carefully been collecting and assembling from the time Allen Sapp first began to paint according to his own vision.

PHOTO: McINTOSH PUBLISHING

Allen Sapp greeting Prime Minister Brian Mulroney at a North Battleford school, 1989

DR. GONOR would regularly receive requests from people all over Canada for information on how to acquire a Sapp painting for presentation to a dignitary — a member of the Royal Family, the prime minister, a retiring governor general — or for a charitable cause.

In 1979, an Allen Sapp painting, *Christmas Evening*, was chosen for inclusion in the UNICEF International Christmas Card Program. Dr. Gonor had been active in UNICEF work for many years, and he had travelled to diverse parts of the world on UNICEF business. The Christmas card was a great success, and Allen was honoured again in 1986, when another of his paintings was chosen for the UNICEF Christmas Card.

HAYSTACK INSIDE WOOD FENCE   *1988   Acrylic on canvas   76.2 cm x 101.6 cm (30" x 40")   Private collection*

When you have horses you should have a good supply of hay.

ON WASH DAY NOKUM LOOKS AFTER THE BABY   *1989   Acrylic on canvas   45.72 cm x 60.96 cm (18" x 24")   Allen Sapp Paintings Inc.*
Before there were electric washing machines, a mother washed the clothes outside and Nokum minded the baby.

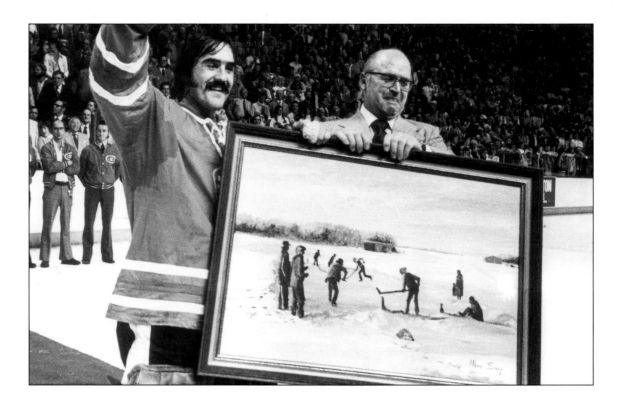

"The 1976 Canada Cup world hockey championship concluded at the Montreal Forum. Sapp was responsible for painting Ice Hockey on the Pond *which was presented to Team Canada netminder Rogatian Vachon."*
– Montreal Star
September 21, 1976

Each year various of Allen's paintings appear on corporate Christmas cards. The Royal Trust Company used his painting *Getting a Drink* on a calendar, which was sent to some 455,000 clients and friends throughout Canada, the United States, and around the world.

While Allen's paintings were gaining wide public acceptance, he was also being recognized and honoured by his peers. In November 1975, he was elected to the Royal Canadian Academy of Arts, in recognition of his outstanding achievement in the field of visual arts. During the same year that Allen Sapp received recognition, Jean-Paul Riopelle, Ken Danby, and Illingworth Kerr, all greatly respected Canadian artists too, were elected to this august body.

On December 5, 1985, Allen Sapp was one of the first recipients of the Saskatchewan Award of Merit, given in recognition of individual excellence and/or contributions to the social and economic well-being of the province and its residents.

Presentation by Her Excellency the Right Honourable Jeanne Sauvé, P. C., C. C., C. M. M., C. D., of the honour Officer of the Order of Canada to Allen Sapp, April 29, 1987

While the protocol officer for the province of Saskatchewan was trying to reach Dr. Gonor to advise him of the most recent honour bestowed on Allen Sapp, word reached Allen in North Battleford that his long-time friend and benefactor had died while travelling in Thailand. Dr. Gonor would, as always, have been proud and happy to hear of Allen Sapp's new success, but it was not to be.

Through all the years, Bill Baker, Allen's manager, worked unobtrusively behind the scenes, looking out for Allen's financial interests. Allen and he spoke frequently by phone, discussing ideas for future paintings, upcoming exhibitions, and often travelled together to gallery showings. Bill built up a network of dealers across North America. He made certain that Allen's paintings not only sold well to a wide audience, but also that Allen was able to be properly compensated for his work. Allen called Bill Baker "my friend," the highest compliment he can offer anyone.

Allen lost another good friend and mentor when, in July 1986, Bill died in Vancouver. He had been contemplating retirement, and there had been fortunately some discussion about his successor. After Bill's passing and talks between Allen Sapp and Ruth Gonor, arrangements were made for John, James, and Monica Kurtz to assume managerial duties for Allen Sapp. The association of the Kurtz family with the artist dates back to 1977, when there was an exhibition in the Assiniboia Gallery, which the Kurtzes own, in Regina to launch the book *A Cree Life: The Art of Allen Sapp*.

Native artists in Canada have had to contend with the attitude in some quarters that their art could be conveniently marginalized because it did not express the aesthetic of the dominant culture. Artistic talent has never been the preserve of any race, colour, or creed, and it is commendable that against long odds artists of native ancestry have made great strides in recent years, joining, on their own terms, the mainstream Canadian artistic community. Still, there are too few native artists represented in the National Gallery of Canada, most native artists only having been added in the past few years.

Fortunately, such omissions have not extended to other areas of society: when Allen Sapp was made an Officer of the Order of Canada in 1987, he was not the first native to join this illustrious group of Canadians.

MEETING WILL START SOON   *1976   Acrylic on canvas   45.72 cm x 60.96 cm (18" x 24")   Allen Sapp Paintings Inc.*
There were some things we would have to talk about, so we would have a meeting at someone's home.

SINGING THE ROUND DANCE SONGS   *1989   Acrylic on canvas   40.64 cm x 50.8 cm (40" x 60")   Allen Sapp Paintings Inc.*

Drummers and singers make a beautiful sound. I especially like the round-dance songs.

When Allen Sapp was to journey to Ottawa for his investiture in the Order of Canada by then governor general Jeanne Sauvé, there were suggestions made not only in Ottawa but in North Battleford also that Allen would have to dress properly, for the invitation to the ceremony read Formal Dress. About the time of his alliance with Dr. Gonor, Allen decided that he would let his hair grow and wear braids and that he would also "dress like an Indian." And ever since, Allen has been known and admired for his Western clothes, denims, bright satin and silk fringed shirts, cowboy boots, and the ever-present black cowboy hat. To receive his honour, Allen dressed as himself, and to say that he stood out at the investiture would be an understatement. But it was a most gratifying moment for him when Madame Sauvé graciously placed the medal around his neck. Allen was pleased to accept the honour, which he described as, "being for all my people."

AFTER THE DEATH of his dear friend and mentor, Dr. Gonor, Allen Sapp, being much more on his own, seemed to develop confidence and became more self-assured. Increasingly open in conversation, he enjoys meeting people at exhibitions and talking about his paintings. In private talks, Allen demonstrates great wisdom as well as keen insight and humour.

In *A Cree Life: The Art of Allen Sapp*, Allen is quoted as saying, "Some people laugh at other people. They should laugh at themselves first. They forget to do that. When someone says bad things, people shouldn't fight back. Just cut it quick. Just sit back and be happy. If you lose money, you can always get it again. If you lose people, they don't come back anymore."

On the 1989 STV program "For Art's Sake" Bill Morrison, the producer, discussed the remark of Allen's just quoted:

There is nothing complicated about what Allen Sapp communicates . . . in his painting and in his life. His love of traditional dance and the challenge of leading and encouraging new generations of Crees to help each other is an old message, but one that personifies the life of this very human artist. There is within this humble spirit a vivid consistency. From the early days of the struggling artist on into a career that has spread his name throughout the world,

Ruth and Allan Gonor

there is little change in this spirit. The simple joy of existence, the sense of stewardship of his people, and his basic humanity seem unspoiled by success.

With his newfound confidence, Allen has been encouraged to speak in public in Cree. When he was invited to be guest speaker at the 4th Wasakaw Pisim Conference in Regina General Hospital in 1987, Allen addressed a crowd of doctors, hospital staff, social workers, and many native people. He spoke in Cree, and he had an interpreter, Gordon Tootoosis. Everything went very smoothly, just as if they had been at a United Nations meeting. Afterward, Allen quipped that he's bilingual: he speaks English and Cree.

Allen has always been interested in helping his people. The topic of the Wasakaw Pisim Conference, a native children's liaison project, was "Paving the Way for Our Youth." After the conference, Allen received a letter from the Wasakaw Pisim staff that read:

EVERYONE'S PLAYING   *1984   Acrylic on canvas   40.64 cm x 50.8 cm (16" x 20")   Allen Sapp Paintings Inc.*
In the summertime it was good to play outside. Both kids and older people liked to play games.

CHARLIE BEAR'S HORSE   *1971   Acrylic on canvas   45.72 cm x 60.96 cm (18" x 24")   Allen Sapp Paintings Inc.*

Charlie Bear's horse was very important to him. He liked him a lot and looked after him well.

We would like to thank you for coming to help us out. In the four conferences we've had, this was the best conference. You helped make it a success. The comments on the evaluation forms were like this: "This information I received today, I'll take and use it to better understand the Indian patient." "It's good to see Indian leaders coming up to motivate young people." "I never knew my own culture or value system, for the first time I'm proud to be an Indian."

In his speech, Allen mentioned that the unique talent he has as an artist has enabled him to do many things for himself and his people. He went on to say that the fact that he was invited to the meeting suggests his own people are proud of him. He urged anyone with the talent or desire to become an artist to pursue the goal, as the rewards are very satisfying.

Continuing, Allen said:

I try to show the hardships and ordeals that my people had to overcome in the past in trying to earn a living. This was made more difficult because of the drastic changes most of them faced in a society which was so different from theirs. They would have to work many hours in the woods cutting wood. Their guns would be at their side, and if they saw some game or prairie chickens, they would try to shoot them so they would have something to take home for food. These are the images I paint — a way of life of my people not too long ago. I paint so my people will have pride in their past and not to think less of themselves. I hope, too, that society generally will have more respect for our heritage.

   Some of the problems in Indian society have been that we have forgotten our culture — we have not kept up our language — the many things that our elders have taught us have been forgotten. We must take the time to talk and help people who have problems, who may be depressed. The young people must be taught our culture; they must know about their rich heritage. It is important that they learn English, but they also should learn Cree — they will have to live in both worlds — but to be happy they must not forget the old ways.

Young people must have an objective in life. They must be encouraged to follow this objective, and not let any disruptions keep them from reaching it.

There are some things like alcohol and drugs which are leading our people in the wrong direction. These are negative forces which keep us from being positive. It would be better if the young people would stay away from alcohol and drugs and realize that they are blessed with a different way of life here, as an Indian. They must have respect for themselves, which alcohol and drugs can only destroy.

Young people must also have respect for the parents and elders. Young people must be willing to learn things from older people. Experience is a good teacher, and this wisdom can be passed on from older people to their children.

Our older people are one of the most important human resources that we have. . . . We must be sure that older people are looked after and not abused. The young people will be much better if they show respect for the elderly. In my paintings I like to depict young people — and young people enjoying life. Both young and old can live a happy life if they learn to respect and get along with one another.

Allen Sapp is very close and loyal to his friends. There are a few other people he jokes with and gets along with, and an additional small number that he tolerates. Although he remembers unpleasant occurrences, he does not dwell on them. Unpleasant matters may come up if someone talks about his early life, but he has had enough good things happen in his later years that his life is almost one continuous high.

Some of the events that have made Allen very happy are becoming an Officer of the Order of Canada and the opening of the Allen Sapp Gallery in North Battleford. Simple events make him just as happy: visiting a Western boot factory close to Trois Rivières, Quebec, and meeting the third generation of the Boulet family who own and operate the factory; speaking in Cree to doctors, social workers, and some of his own people at the Regina General Hospital; riding in the Calgary Stampede Parade.

LITTLE POW-WOW DANCER   *1969*   *Acrylic on canvas*   *50.8 cm x 40.64 cm (20" x 16")*   *Allen Sapp Paintings Inc.*

Children like to be dressed in fancy costumes and learn to dance when they are small. It helps them to remember who they are.

Allen is not overly impressed with fancy social functions, and feels "high-brow" affairs are "a lot of make-believe." He is, however, always eager to see new places and meet new people; not having the advantage of being able to read and not being an avid fan of television, he finds that his main contact with the world at large comes from meeting new people. He loves to socialize with his own people at pow-wows, and at gallery openings he likes to visit with white people who admire and buy his paintings, and he enjoys the people he meets during his everyday life in North Battleford. He also loves to stop by the Allen Sapp Gallery almost every day and talk to the people viewing the collection of his paintings on display.

He speaks fondly of his grandmother, of his father and of his mother. Pride swells in his voice as he tells of his nephew Alwyn, who is in charge of building and carpentry at the Little Pine reserve. Another nephew, John, is active in chuck-wagon racing, and he has encouraged nephew Dwayne, who has some artistic ability, to keep on drawing.

Allen is concerned about the social problems of his people and, as a lifelong non-drinker, has some strong feelings on the evils of drinking, which he refers to as "stupid" behaviour.

THERE WERE MANY FACETS to the relationship between Allen Sapp and Allan Gonor, but one of the most satisfying chapters culminated with the opening, on May 6, 1989, of the Allen Sapp Gallery — The Gonor Collection, in the refurbished library building in North Battleford. This event was the fulfillment of a dream of Allan Gonor's. He had been so enthusiastic about the work of Allen Sapp, so involved in his career, that at every opportunity he shared his knowledge of the artist and promoted his work in almost every corner of the world.

As Irwin McIntosh wrote in the *North Battleford News Optimist* (November 28, 1975):

The two prove that people can work together sharing their talents to conquer old ideas and traditions. . . . The Allen Sapp and Allan Gonor story will be retold for generations. The brotherhood of man does transcend the ravages of history. . . . Gonor and Sapp have welded new bonds of understanding for all of us.

Over the years, Allan Gonor purchased many, many paintings from Allen Sapp, so in addition to documenting the artist's life on film, tape, and in writing, Dr. Gonor also documented his career by collecting paintings from its every phase. Ruth and Allan Gonor wished that someday their collection of Sapp paintings and the entire Sapp archive would become public property, a legacy for all to enjoy.

At the time Dr. Gonor's death, plans had been in the works for a place to display all the Gonors' material, and soon arrangements were finalized for the City of North Battleford to accept the donation of eighty Allen Sapp paintings, which would be the nucleus of the Allen Sapp Gallery — The Gonor Collection. It is a tribute to the foresight of the City of North Battleford that the city council, under Mayor Glen Hornick, made provision to renovate the old Carnegie Library in order to house the collection in suitable surroundings. The Allen Sapp Gallery is completely modern, with state-of-the-art equipment, and may well be the only gallery in North America established to show the works of an important living artist and dedicated to the memory of an enterprising, imaginative Canadian art lover.

Writing in the *Regina Leader Post* (November 25, 1989), Max Macdonald described the Allen Sapp Gallery — The Gonor Collection:

> North Battleford has built a monument to a local boy who made good, without leaving home, and against odds that would glaze the eyes of a Las Vegas numbers whiz.
>
> This boy is a once-sickly Cree from the Red Pheasant Reserve, a former welfare recipient, who can neither read nor write, and has had no formal art training. Yet he has gained international recognition as a communicator through acrylic on canvas.
>
> This is the triumph of Allen Sapp, fellow of the Royal Canadian Academy of Arts, recipient of the Saskatchewan Award of Merit, and Officer of the Order of Canada.
>
> Now, an additional honor. The city which once eyed him with suspicion as he peddled his paintings on the street has spent about $700,000 to house a collection of his works.

PHOTO: OWEN EINSIEDLER

Allen Sapp, Ruth Gonor, and Curator Dean Bauche in front of the Allen Sapp Gallery — The Gonor Collection, 1989

The Allen Sapp Gallery opened in early May. By mid-November more than 7500 visitors had come to explore the life of Sapp and a collection of works, which the late Dr. Allan Gonor and his widow, Ruth, donated to the city in public trust.

That the gallery ever came into being is in itself a triumph for civic administrators. A project of this magnitude is a major undertaking for a city of 15,000. However, a number of elements were in place to make it work.

First, Gonor, who was a major influence in the artist's story, felt his extensive collection of Sapp paintings should in some way or another be turned over to the public.

Meanwhile, an idea was percolating in the minds of North Battleford Mayor Jim Maher, and City Commissioner Ab Bridges. When the old Carnegie Library was replaced by a new facility, the two had exploratory talks with Gonor about using part of the old building for some sort of "Sapp Museum."

Thus it was upon Gonor's death in 1985 that when his widow, Ruth, approached the city fathers they were ready to listen. Even though Maher had been replaced by Mayor Glen Hornick, and Doug McEwan was appointed City Commissioner, the project easily survived.

The Gonor commission of eighty of Sapp's works, ranging over his entire career, were turned over to the city on condition that they not be sold, that they be for public display and housed in a facility to properly protect them.

With 743 square metres of space on two floors, a full-time curator, Dean Bauche, and two or three part-timers, the gallery has become one of the city's most popular tourist attractions. It draws not only art lovers, but those interested in examining the cultural life of the Cree in which Sapp is still an active participant.

THE FINAL CHAPTER in the Allen Sapp Story has not yet been written. Although the artist has achieved great success and received wide acclaim, much more than most artists during their lives, History and Time will record the value of his works and the contributions he has made to the heritage of his people. As is the case with the paintings of other great Canadian artists, the passage of time only will make his works more desirable and the thoughts he has expressed in his paintings more beautiful.

The paintings of Allen Sapp. The inspiration of Allan Gonor. Two spirits soar — and we have a legacy of friendship and commitment to appreciate and emulate.

WYNONA MULCASTER'S KEYNOTE SPEECH
AT THE ALLEN SAPP GALLERY OPENING
MAY 6, 1989

AFTERWORD

*Wynona Mulcaster and Allen Sapp at the opening of the
Allen Sapp Gallery — The Gonor Collection*

PHOTO: WARWICK PUBLICATIONS INC., NORTH BATTLEFORD

Transcribed by Ann Knight

*A HIGHLIGHT OF THE OPENING of the Allen Sapp Gallery — The Gonor Collection was
Wynona Mulcaster's keynote speech. Mulcaster had arrived from Mexico, where she now
resides, just in time for the opening. She has had an important place in the life of Allen
Sapp, and her joy at being asked to give the address at the gallery opening is evident in
her words.*

WHO KNEW TWENTY YEARS AGO that down the road there would be a day like this?

Allan Gonor came through my door with that radiant enthusiasm, his eyes
aglow, which many of you in North Battleford remember him for. Behind him
came that tall, quiet, dignified man, Allen Sapp, without a flicker of expression on
his face. He and I looked at each other. It summed up as "Well, who are *you*?"

Allan Gonor took out a stack of paintings and started to lay them out on my studio floor. At first, I was aghast. Sapp obviously had a photographic memory and a
good, skilled hand. And he had obviously been through Woolworth's and all the
gift shops and he had seen the paintings of Indian children with teardrops coming
down their faces, and he was able to go home and repeat those subjects exactly.

He had seen the landscapes you know so well from the hardware stores — where there's a mountain in the middle and a deer on this side, and a deer on that side, and a lake in the middle. You know the kind. He could just turn them out like that.

I looked at these and I thought, Dear me, what can I do for this man?

But then, there was one painting that was down on the floor. It was a log shack with a sod roof. And in front was a pile of wood. On the chopping block, there was an axe that had just split a piece of wood. You could almost feel the crack of the wood as it split. And I used to like chopping wood when I was young. It's a great thing to do. Try it sometime.

Allen had caught the feeling in that painting. And I took all my courage in my hands to be frankly honest. And I said, "Allen, all these are garbage. This [one] is the painting; this is the kind of painting you should do."

And he looked a little worried when I said, "You must paint the Indian way of life. You must paint the way your people feel. Paint the experiences you have had as an Indian."

He said, "I don't think my people would like that."

And I said, "Why would they not like it?"

He said, "They might laugh at us."

I said firmly, "No!"

And Allan Gonor said, "No, they will not laugh. They will love it. This is what the people want. You must use your experiences to paint."

Art is a language. It's not a skill. It's not a stunt. It's not something that you just learn to do and put it down. It comes from the heart.

While he was copying pictures from other sources, there was nothing of Allen in the work. And so we started a long series. Every Saturday for a year, Dr. Allan Gonor brought Allen Sapp to my studio and we spent Saturday mornings together.

And I learned to have a great respect and admiration for this fine and strong, talented man.

You can't teach art any more than you can grow roses. You can make the ground right. The rose has to produce. And I tried to make the ground right for Allen, because he had no experience with what was good art and what was just making pictures. There's a big difference. At first, he had not the language of art. And I had to learn to put understandings of a subtle nature into terms that he and I both understood. It was very exciting for me to see how he did understand, and how his paintings developed from just making pictures, into making art — which is the language of life.

I can remember that every Saturday he would bring out a whole stack of paintings from the trunk of Allan Gonor's car, and he would lay them out on the lawn and we would discuss them. I could honestly say that I was deeply moved.

I can remember one picture in particular that he produced, and I looked at it and my heart stood still. Tears came into my eyes and I said, "Allen, it is very sad." I knew that it was his grandmother.

He said nothing for a long time. He stood quietly beside me, and then he said, "She's dead." That was a very close moment.

There are times when artists reach a peak experience. (Artists don't always paint masterpieces. No artist does.) But there are times when the spirit moves and the painting makes its own demands, and it almost happens by itself. It's a magic moment that every artist prays for. (And some never get; and some get only seldom.) Allen had these magic moments when he produced masterpieces.

As the world becomes more discriminating and sees the difference between great art and mediocre art, I believe that Allen will be more and more treasured in the world of art because he has produced many masterpieces.

Now this could not have happened without the dedication of Dr. Gonor. Many people start with projects and lose interest. But Dr. Gonor was dedicated. He was there every Saturday, full of enthusiasm. He never waivered. And behind was that staunch, wise, wonderful Ruth, who played a bigger part in that whole picture than probably most people realize. What a fine pair they were.

When I think that Allen Sapp grew up in a so-called civilized community, that he was allowed to grow up (and be in hospital for a period of time with a serious illness) and was not taught to read or to write, that he was never given an opportunity to develop this precious gift, I think we must face this, and realize that not only Indian children but white children are also facing this deprivation [today], and are not having the opportunity to develop their natural gifts. Our greatest natural resource is the creativity of our young people. We should think seriously about this and not allow it to continue.

After Allen had painted with me a little more than a year, he had his first exhibition. He had been peddling his paintings, selling them for five dollars apiece. I put thirty easels up in my garden, invited Saskatoon to come, and they flocked out to see Allen's first exhibition. They were excited. A storm blew up. And it started to rain.

We gathered all the paintings quickly up and put them in my carport. Dr. Gonor climbed up on a barrel and starting lifting the paintings and showing them to the people one at at time. And he was selling paintings, for [up to] $1500. I thought Allen would faint. I was so excited. Immediately Sapp's reputation became known. He was launched. He was off. It was very exciting. And I'm very proud to have had a small part in it.

I did not teach Allen. He had it all inside him. I think I helped it to come out.

I know the sun is hot and I was told I should not talk for more than fifteen minutes, but I must say that I think what you have done in North Battleford is a big thing. Like dropping a pebble in a pool, the ripples flow out and out. I believe that the planet is in the process of transformation. There is a network of re-evaluation going on over the whole world. I believe that thirty years ago this could not have happened. But I believe there is a new sense of values being developed across the world, and you are a part. We can't wait for governments to do anything for us. The time has come when we individuals and individual communities must do things for themselves — and it spreads from one community to another. And I believe that you are one of the communities that are making things happen. I am sure that there are more Allan Gonors and Ruth Gonors among you who will see that this sort of thing continues.

Not only will this be a tourist attraction, but it will bring the native people closer to us [the whites]. They have so much to teach us. My great respect goes to them, to Allen, and to North Battleford. God bless you.

INDEX TO ILLUSTRATIONS

Height precedes width on reproductions.

SELECTED BIBLIOGRAPHY AND FILMOGRAPHY

Bauche, D. G. "'Naheyow' A Portrait of Allen Sapp and His People," Allen Sapp Gallery — The Gonor Collection, North Battleford, 1989.

Bradshaw, Thecla (Zeeh). *Recent Paintings by Allen Sapp*. Exhibition catalogue, Mendel Gallery, Saskatoon, 1969.

Department of Indian and Northern Affairs (produced for). *The Colours Of Pride*, National Film Board of Canada, 1973.

Earl, Marjorie. "Wonders of the Prairies Haunt Allen Sapp Art Book" *Winnipeg Tribune*, November 8, 1977.

Hammer, Victor. *Allen Sapp: By Instinct a Painter*. Exhibition catalogue, Hammer Galleries, New York, New York, 1976.

Harrison, Julia D., Ruth Holmes Whitehead, Ruth B. Phillips, Ted J. Brasser, Judy Thompson, Bernadette Driscoll, and Martine Reid. *The Spirit Sings: Artistic Traditions of Canada's First Peoples*. McClelland and Stewart, Toronto, and Glenbow Museum, Calgary, 1987.

Loercher, Diana. "A Uniquely Indian Vision — In Manhattan," *Christian Science Monitor*, May 5, 1976.

Lovoos, Janice. "Allen Sapp, Cree Indian Artist," *Southwest Art 4* (7), 1979.

MacDonald, Max. "Home Town Recognition Touches Artist's Heart," *Regina Leader Post*, November 25, 1989.

MacEwan, Grant. *Portraits from the Plains*. McGraw-Hill Co. of Canada, Toronto, 1971.

McIntosh, Irwin. "The Making of a Great Artist," *North Battleford News Optimist*, November 28, 1975.

McLuhan, Elizabeth. *Tailfeathers/Sapp/Janvier: Selections from the Art Collection of the Glenbow Museum*. Thunder Bay Art Gallery, Thunder Bay, 1982.

Morrison, Bill (producer). "For Art's Sake," *Allen Sapp*, STV Saskatoon, 1989.

Perry, Meta. "Regina Exhibition Shows Changes in Acclaimed Artist Sapp," *Regina Leader Post*, November 14, 1985.

Podedworny, Carol. *Eight from the Prairies*, Exhibition catalogue, Thunder Bay Art Gallery, Thunder Bay, 1987.

Robertson, Sheila. "Allen Sapp Celebrated As Hero in North Battleford", *Saskatoon Star-Phoenix*, May 6, 1989.

———. "Sapp Sees Art As Reflection of Cree Life for Posterity" *Saskatoon Star Phoenix*, January 24, 1987.

Warner, John Anson. "The Cree Artist Allen Sapp," *The Beaver*, Winter 1973.

———. "Allen Sapp, Cree Painter" *American Indian Art*, 2 (1) 1976.

———. and Bradshaw, Thecla. *A Cree Life: The Art of Allen Sapp* J. J. Douglas, Vancouver, 1977.

Wigmore, Donnalu (producer). *Four Prairie Artists*, CBC Television, 1983.

Zborowsky, Bill (producer). *By Instinct a Painter*, CBC Television, 1971.

ALLEN SAPP'S DEALERS

Over the past twenty years, Allen Sapp has exhibited with numerous galleries across Canada and in the United States and Europe. These galleries have brought the paintings of Allen Sapp into the lives of countless collectors and admirers through their one-person exhibitions and their continuing efforts at representing his work. Currently the works of Allen Sapp may be found at the following commercial galleries:

Agassiz Gallery, Winnipeg, Manitoba
Agghazy Art Agency, Sidney, British Columbia
Assiniboia Gallery, Regina, Saskatchewan
Assiniboia Bessborough Gallery, Saskatoon, Saskatchewan
Beckett Gallery, Hamilton, Ontario
Clinton Court Gallery, North Battleford, Saskatchewan
Continental Gallery, Montréal, Québec
Elayne Galleries, Minneapolis, Minnesota
Gallery Indigena, Waterloo, Ontario
Hollander York Gallery, Toronto, Ontario
Humberston Edwards Fine Art, West Vancouver, British Columbia
Lourie Gallery, Toronto, Ontario
Masters Gallery, Calgary, Alberta
Robertson Gallery, Ottawa, Ontario
The Gallery, St. John's, Newfoundland
Trailside Galleries, Jackson Hole, Wyoming
Woltjen-Udell Gallery, Edmonton, Alberta